LIFE AT THE ABBEY

SPLENDID REMAINS

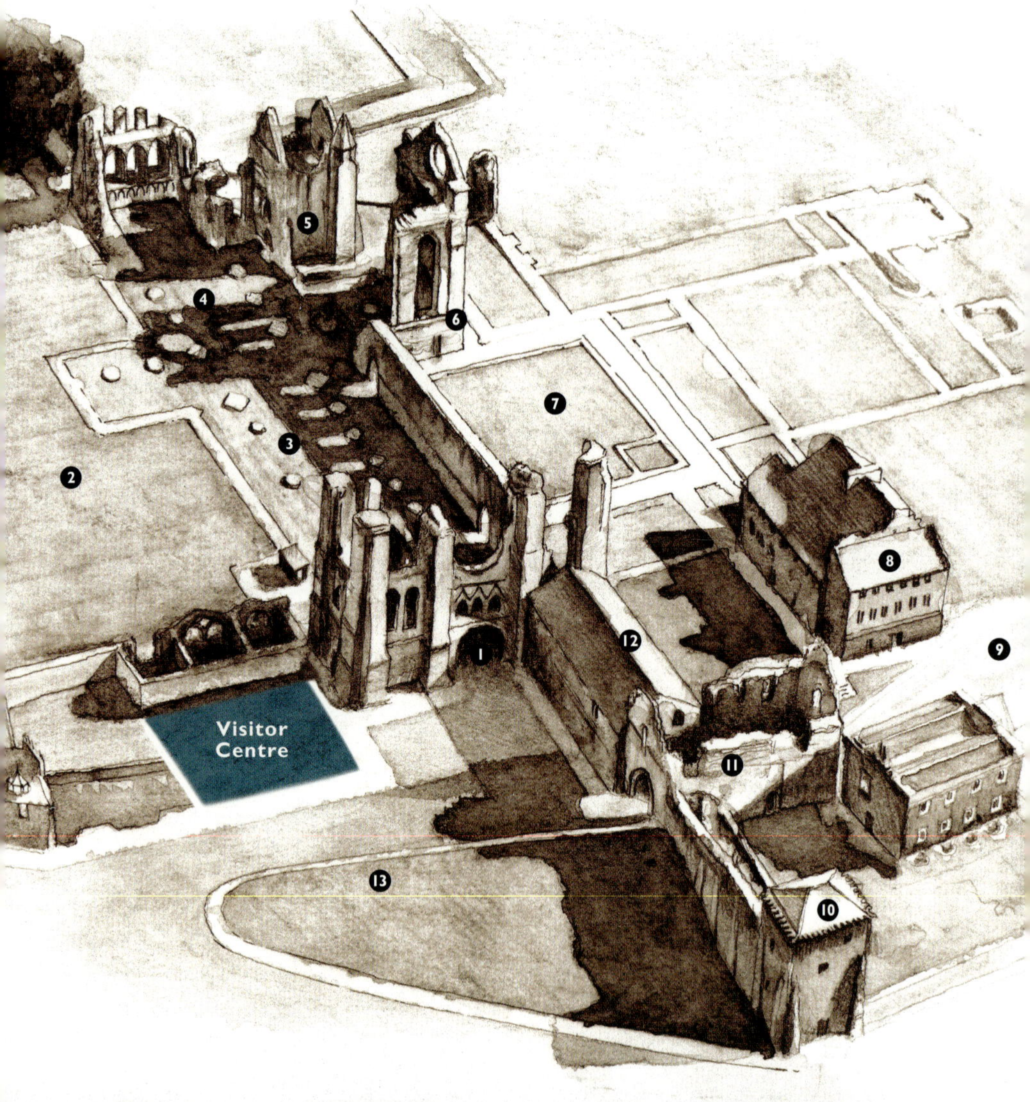

2

5

4

6

7

3

8

9

12

10

11

1

Visitor Centre

13

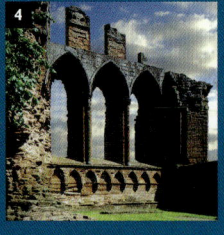

WELCOME TO ARBROATH ABBEY

'A ncient magnificence' was how Dr Johnson described the ruins of Arbroath Abbey when he visited it in 1773. King William I, 'the Lion', founded the monastery in 1178 in memory of his boyhood friend St Thomas Becket, murdered in Canterbury Cathedral eight years earlier. William invited Tironensian monks from Kelso Abbey, near the English border, to settle in Arbroath, and before his own death in 1214 chose to be buried at the abbey.

Above: The abbey seal, depicting the martyrdom of St Thomas Becket, to whom the abbey was dedicated.

Arbroath Abbey is rightly famed for its place in Scotland's national consciousness – most memorably for the Declaration of Arbroath. Written in April 1320 by one of the clerks under Abbot Bernard of Arbroath, King Robert I's chancellor, the Declaration articulated the right of the Scottish people to freedom from English interference.

CONTENTS

Left: The famous Declaration of Arbroath, Scotland's declaration of independence, was composed at the abbey in 1320.

ARBROATH ABBEY AT A GLANCE

Time and weather have not been kind to Arbroath Abbey, one of the finest monasteries of medieval Scotland. While the abbey flourished for nearly 400 years, it fell into a steep decline after the Protestant Reformation of 1560. Today, much of the monks' cloister, placed on the sunny south side of the abbey church, has gone, and the great church itself survives only in fragments.

But what superb fragments! They allow us to imagine the splendour of Arbroath Abbey after its completion in 1233, as well as the lives of the men who prayed, worked and lived in its confines. At its height Arbroath was one of the richest monasteries in Scotland, deriving an income from royal and aristocratic land grants as well as about 35 parish churches.

Right: The town of Arbroath owes its history to the abbey, whose ageing ruins (left) dominate this hand-coloured version of John Slezer's 1678 view. The harbour (far right) was built and maintained by the abbots.

POWERFUL PEOPLE

9 ABBOT PANITER
Abbot Walter Paniter built the sacristy onto the abbey church in the mid-1400s and led a movement to improve standards in Scotland's Benedictine monasteries.

18 WILLIAM THE LION
William I, 'the Lion', founded Arbroath Abbey as part of his efforts to extend his control throughout Scotland. Other measures included granting charters to many burghs (towns).

25 CARDINAL BEATON
A towering figure in Scottish politics before the Reformation, the cardinal was one of three members of the Beaton family to hold the office of abbot of Arbroath.

HIGH POLITICS

18 BECKET MURDER

The assassination in 1170 of Thomas Becket, archbishop of Canterbury, gave William I spiritual and political motives for founding Arbroath.

22 DECLARATION OF ARBROATH

Scotland's very own declaration of independence was composed at the abbey under the direction of Abbot Bernard, Robert I's chancellor.

25 ROYAL APPOINTEES
The abbey's fortunes waned even before the Reformation when, after 1500, the post of abbot became more a source of income than a position of spiritual leadership.

A GUIDED TOUR

The abbey church at Arbroath, one of the most impressive churches in medieval Scotland, was around 90m long, and its three towers – one over the central crossing (now gone) and two at the west front – must have seemed to offer a foretaste of the heavenly Jerusalem to all who gazed on them.

The imposing twin-towered west front still soars high into the sky, whilst the presbytery, choir and south transept, where most of the main services took place, retains some of the finest early Gothic architecture to be seen in Scotland. Next to the cloister is the abbot's house, one of the most complete abbot's residences in Britain, and close by it a striking stretch of precinct wall.

Above: Unlike much else at Arbroath, the abbot's house survived the Reformation largely intact because it was capable of reuse.

Below: The circular window in the south transept's gable – known locally as the 'Round O'.

Illustration key

1	West front	12	Guest house
2	Monks' cemetery	13	Outer precinct
3	Nave		
4	Presbytery and choir		
5	Sacristy		
6	South transept		
7	Cloister		
8	Abbot's house		
9	Inner precinct		
10	Regality Tower		
11	Gatehouse		

THE ABBEY CHURCH

The west front of the church was designed to offer a magnificent first impression of this great royal monastery. Towers were an important element in the medieval idea of architectural splendour, and the grandest churches usually had a symmetrical pair flanking the main entrance, as well as a further tower over the centre of the church. The great abbey of Dunfermline, founded by William I's grandfather, David I, was possibly the first church in Scotland to have such a triplet of towers. William may have been hoping that Arbroath would replace Dunfermline as the royal mausoleum – it certainly became his own burial place.

The two flanking towers were originally identical, but damage caused by a violent storm in 1272 led to the north tower being heightened. No structural evidence remains for this extra level, but it can be seen in late 18th-century illustrations of the abbey.

Above: An engraving of 1790 depicting the abbey church from the outer precinct. The great west doorway was used only on special occasions, such as the anniversary of William I's death (4 December). Since this engraving was published, parts of the two tall western towers have collapsed.

THE NAVE

The nine-bay nave, flanked by side aisles along its full length, was the only part of the church accessible to the laity, whose parish church was at St Vigeans, a mile to the north. The monks used the nave when processing to their choir. The best-preserved section is at the north-west corner, which gives us a good idea of how the three-storeyed nave would have looked. At the lowest level is a tall arcade of arches opening into the flanking aisles. Above the arcade were pairs of arches that opened into the gallery below the roofs over the aisles. The third level was the clearstorey, a line of windows bringing light into the nave.

A striking feature of the outer wall of the south nave aisle is that its lower part is more roughly built than the upper part. This detail may indicate that there was a less ambitious first design for the abbey in 1178. When the grander scheme was adopted, the nave and the cloister may well have been extended eastwards by one bay.

Above: A view looking eastwards down the nave towards the choir and presbytery.

'It has three naves, the largest in the middle, and the lesser at the sides. The centre nave is roofed with wood. It is covered in the main part with lead, and the rest of it with wooden shingles. It has a splendid tower, with four sides, and it has many most excellent bells.'

A description of the nave by Arthur Boece, a priest in the diocese of Brechin, in 1517.

THE SOUTH TRANSEPT

The architectural richness that Arbroath clearly displayed is seen to most striking effect in the south transept. Because its gable wall adjoined the two-storeyed east cloister range, there could only be windows in the upper part, above the dormitory roof, but there was no question of the lower walls being simply left blank. Here are three tiers of decorative arcading, each slightly different. The lower two were simply set against the wall, their arches carried on free-standing single or paired shafts (now gone). The third tier opened onto a wall

Above: The sacristy (left) and south transept (right), from a 19th-century watercolour by Robert Billings. The sacristy, the only roofed part of the abbey church to survive, is well known for its acoustics.

passage from which there was access to the monks' dormitory through a doorway – a spiral stair leading down from this passage served as the monks' access to the church for the night-time services. Above the arcading is a pair of tall windows, their sides pierced by more wall passages.

In the gable is Arbroath's most notable landmark, the large circular window known locally as the 'Round O'. It was used as a navigational landmark long after the last monk had died. In 1809 the engineer Robert Stevenson – the grandfather of novelist Robert Louis Stevenson – rebuilt the Round O during his construction of the Bell Rock lighthouse, 11 miles (18km) off Arbroath.

Below: One of two aumbries (cupboards) in the sacristy. A worn coat-of-arms above it is that of Walter Paniter, abbot from 1411 to 1449.

THE SACRISTY

The sacristy was where priests prepared for services and stored their vestments, books and other liturgical items. The original sacristy may only have been a partitioned-off space within the church, but a purpose-built sacristy was added to the south choir aisle in the mid-1400s by Abbot Walter Paniter.

The lower walls have decorative arcading, apart from the east wall, where there would probably have been an altar. Three aumbries (wall cupboards) and a small chamber in the south-west corner stored the more precious items. In the 18th century this chamber was used to contain declared lunatics, and was named 'Jenny Batter's Hole' after the last occupant. The spiral stair, giving access to what would have been a treasury on the upper floor, could only be reached through elevated doorways, which required ladders for access.

'The sacristy, at the south side of the choir, possesses a silver cross, very many chalices, other vessels and silver images of the saints, also many suits of vestments, of gold and of silk. In it are also preserved a pastoral staff and a mitre.'

A description of the sacristy by Arthur Boece in 1517.

Right: This 14th-century six-arced cup, on display at the abbey's visitor centre, may have been stored in the sacristy, although it is more likely that it was used as a drinking vessel.

THE PRESBYTERY AND CHOIR

The east end of the church housed the most liturgically important elements, the high altar in the presbytery and the monks' stalls in the choir. Because of their significance, these were the first parts of the church to be built. However, very little of what we see dates from before the closing years of the 12th century, raising again the possibility that an earlier, smaller church was originally envisaged in 1178 (see page 7).

The presbytery, the most sacred part of the church, would have been bathed in light, since there were windows on three sides and no flanking aisles. The east wall, terminating the view down the length of the church, would have been the most imposing part, with three tiers of triplets of windows (two tiers of which survive), above which was perhaps a rose window in the gable.

The choir has largely gone. The location for an altar at the east end of the south aisle is indicated by the arched double piscina (stone basin) in the adjacent south wall; the sacred vessels used at mass were washed here. There is also an aumbry, where items for use in the mass could be placed. The monks' wooden choir stalls would have been set against the arcade piers, of which only the stumps remain.

Right: The east end of the presbytery. A fragment of the high altar lies a short distance from the wall. William I was buried in front of this altar on 10 December 1214.

Left: A detail from a retable (decorated screen), depicting five female saints, on display at the abbot's house. Retables such as this would have graced the abbey church's numerous altars.

'The high altar is situated at the top of the church, near the east, at a little distance from the wall, and on it daily two, and frequently three, masses are celebrated with the chant. On the altar, for an ornament, there is a wooden tabernacle, gilt, in which are these sculptured images: the Saviour having the world in his hand; St Mary, the mother of God, with the child Jesus in her bosom; St Thomas the martyr; and King William offering the church. Round the altar is a wooden choir, with a double row of stalls.'

A description of the high altar by Arthur Boece in 1517.

THE CLOISTER AND INNER PRECINCT

The cloister was a rectangular open court around which were the buildings in which the monks lived. Possibly because of its great wealth, Arbroath had a second courtyard to the south of the cloister. However, the basic arrangement, common to most monasteries, is much as would be expected.

The east range consisted of the parlour, a passage beside the church leading out to the wider precinct, and where the monks could converse. Next to it was the chapter house, the most important room in the cloister, where monks discussed business. South of the chapter house was the warming house, where the monks were permitted the luxury of a social fireplace.

Above: The remains of the cloister complex, viewed from the site of the east range. Most of the cloister was demolished after the Reformation of 1560. Some of the outlying buildings, such as the infirmary, have disappeared without trace.

One of the rooms beyond may have been the novices' room, where those aspiring to become monks were taught. At first-floor level along the entire east range would have been the dormitory.

The south range housed the refectory (dining hall) and kitchens. Before entering the refectory, the monks cleansed their hands at the lavatorium (water basin), housed in a small pavilion at the south-west corner of the cloister. Arthur Boece tells of two refectories, one for common days and one for feasts. It is likely that the second refectory was a 'misericord', where monks were allowed to eat meat, which was normally forbidden.

Little can be made of the west range, other than the outer parlour, next to the church, with slight traces of its ribbed barrel vault and wall cupboards. Since this range was closest to the main gateway into the inner precinct, it probably provided accommodation and storage for the cellarer, the monk responsible for provisioning the house.

Below: A reconstruction of what Arbroath Abbey might have looked like before the Reformation, depicting the cloister complex and inner precinct.

Illustration key

1	Cloister	11	Gatehouse range
2	Chapter house	12	Regality Tower
3	East range	13	Outer precinct
4	Little cloister		
5	Refectory		
6	Kitchens		
7	West range		
8	Abbot's house		
9	Inner precinct		
10	Guest house		

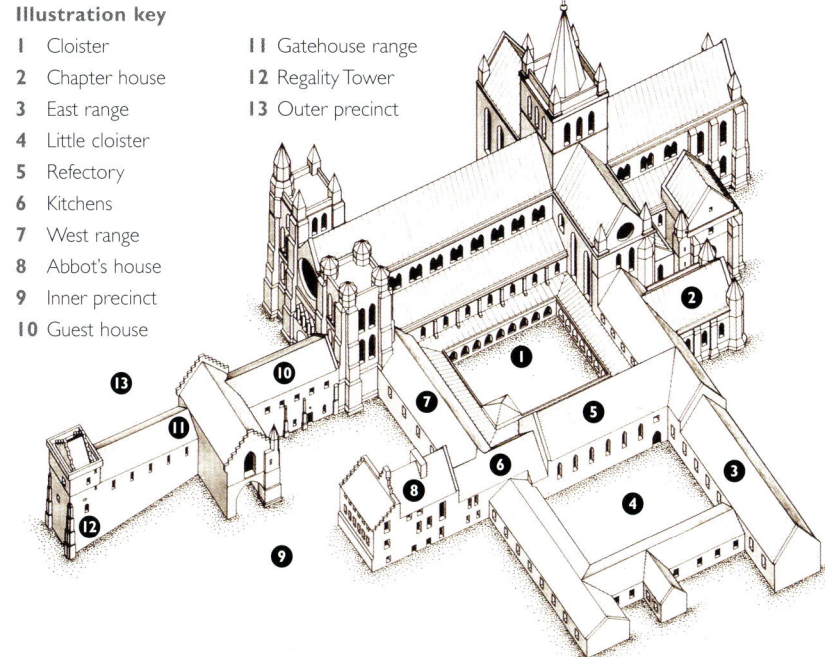

THE ABBOT'S HOUSE

Although abbots were expected to live in common with their fellow monks, because of the many demands made upon them they tended to live in residences set a little apart from the rest. One common solution was to locate the house in the west range, where they were closest to the outside world. This is what happened at Arbroath.

The nucleus of the original abbot's house was a two-storeyed block projecting from the south-west corner of the cloister; it still survives in modified form at the core of the present structure. The architectural details suggest that it was built around 1200. The building had a large stone-vaulted room at ground level and, on the upper floor, a more lofty private chamber with a timber roof and lancet windows. There may have been other rooms within the west range, including perhaps a hall.

Above: This 16th-century carving may have formed part of the panelling in the abbot's house (top).

The house was greatly extended in the early to mid-1500s, becoming more self-contained. The main accommodation was at first-floor level, where traces of painted decoration hint at the internal splendour of the finished house. The ground floor seems to have been made into a kitchen, judging by the large fireplace built in its west wall.

Unlike the rest of the cloister, the abbot's house survived the destruction of the post-Reformation era thanks to its use firstly as a manse for the parish minister and then as a thread factory and a school. It stands today as one of the most complete abbot's residences in Britain.

Above: The stone vaulting in the ground floor of the abbot's house gives an idea of the building's original interiors.

THE GATEHOUSE RANGE

Across from the abbot's house is a two-storeyed building that may have been the guest house, where important visitors were accommodated. The two ground-floor rooms could have formed a two-roomed apartment, consisting of a hall and a smaller bedchamber. The upper floor (now entered from inside the abbey church) is currently one space but may have been subdivided.

The gatehouse, to the west, was one of the most imposing monastery entrances in Scotland, comparable to that at St Andrews Cathedral. Beyond it was another range behind the impressive precinct wall (not at present accessible), which may have housed offices for the regality court, the body that administered the abbey's vast estates. The so-called Regality Tower at the end of the range has four floors, arranged similarly to a Scottish laird's tower house, except that the rooms are smaller. The tower, which is not open to visitors, has clearly undergone many changes, and latterly may have provided apartments for senior monks.

Above: The front of the gatehouse entrance (foreground) looks south onto the inner precinct. It was originally secured by a portcullis.

THE STORY OF
ARBROATH ABBEY

The story of the monks of Arbroath Abbey began in France in about 1105. In that year Abbot Bernard left the abbey of St Cyprien, in Poitiers, to form a new monastery. He eventually alighted on a place called Tiron, from which his new order took its name.

The Tironensians, a reformed order of Benedictine monks, soon attracted the attention of the saintly Prince David of Scotland, who in about 1113 invited them to establish an abbey at Selkirk. By the time they relocated to Kelso in about 1128, to be closer to the royal castle of Roxburgh, Prince David was ruling as King David I.

David's successors maintained a particular affection for the Tironensians, perhaps partly because the order was only minimally represented in England. David himself established another abbey at Lesmahagow, whilst one of his grandsons, David earl of Huntingdon, founded Lindores Abbey in about 1190. But the most magnificently endowed Tironensian house in Scotland was to be that at Arbroath, established in 1178 by another of David's grandsons, King William I.

Above: An illumination from the charter of the Tironensian abbey at Kelso, depicting its founder, David I. His grandson, William I, founded Arbroath Abbey for the Tironensians about 50 years later.

Opposite left: A Billings watercolour of the west front and north-west tower, viewed from the south aisle of the nave.

TIMELINE

c.1105

A NEW ORDER EMERGES
Abbot Bernard founds the Tironensian order of monks at Tiron, near Chartres.

c.1113

THE TIRONENSIANS IN SCOTLAND
The Tironensians establish Selkirk Abbey (later moved to Kelso, right), the first foundation by reformed Benedictines in Britain.

FOUNDING THE ABBEY

T he main reason for William I's foundation of Arbroath appears to have been his fear that he had incurred divine wrath by invading England in 1174. The invasion was a disaster for the king, resulting in his capture at Alnwick. According to contemporary accounts, this capture occurred at the precise moment Henry II of England was seeking forgiveness for having prompted the assassination of Thomas Becket, the archbishop of Canterbury, in 1170.

Left: The murder of Archbishop Thomas Becket, depicted in a psalter illustration of c.1220. One of the assassins was a son of Hugh de Morville, constable of Scotland and founder of Dryburgh Abbey.

William and Thomas had been boyhood friends, and in an age that placed great emphasis on supernatural coincidences, the king's capture suggested that his dead friend – canonised the previous year – was not pleased with his aggressive action. It is likely, however, that William founded the abbey for more than this reason alone. Thomas's continued role as a thorn in Henry's side would certainly have appealed to William, whilst on a more practical level an abbey at Arbroath was one way of reinforcing royal authority in the northern part of his kingdom.

Construction work began almost immediately, although possibly at first on a smaller scale. The church we now see was perhaps started a little before 1200. At few other Scottish churches is there such clear evidence of a major building being completed in the course of a relatively brief operation. Enough of the east end must have been finished for the burial there of William himself, in 1214. The church was dedicated for worship on 8 May 1233.

The church was so large and architecturally splendid that it required relatively few structural changes throughout the rest of its history. Routine maintenance work, of course, was necessary from time to time. In 1474 Stephen Liel, a carpenter from St Andrews, was contracted to carry out work on the abbey and its dependent parish churches for an annual fee of 20 merks.

Below: The Monymusk Reliquary, on display at the Museum of Scotland in Edinbugh. It was once believed to be the Breccbennach (said to hold relics of St Columba), which was granted to Arboath by William I, as a sign of royal favour.

1178

A SAINTLY FOUNDATION
William I invites the Tironensians to Arbroath and dedicates their abbey to his friend St Thomas Becket.

1214

A ROYAL BURIAL
William I dies in Stirling on 4 December. His body is interred in front of Arbroath's high altar six days later.

DAILY LIFE

Monasteries existed primarily to serve as beacons of prayer in a sinful world. The basis of the routine was the *opus dei* (work of God), a daily round of services that started perhaps as early as 1.30 a.m. in the summer, and ended when the monks retired to their dormitory at about 8.30 p.m. The sequence of services – Matins, Lauds, Prime, Terce, Sext, None, Vespers and Compline – consisted of psalms, readings, prayers and antiphons. Additionally, there were usually at least two corporate celebrations of the mass, and private masses at the side altars, of which we know there were 12 at Arbroath in 1517.

In the intervals between services, the monks were expected to undertake work of various kinds, including spiritual work. St Bernard of Tiron, the founder of the order of monks at Arbroath, had recommended manual work as a way of keeping idle hands out of mischief, although this probably meant craftwork as opposed to hard physical labour. Some of this work involved producing and maintaining books, and Arbroath is known to have possessed a distinguished library, a partial inventory of which survives from 1473.

Above: This beautifully carved 14th-century figure was found in 1815 in the north-west tower. In 1396 Pope Benedict XIII granted the abbots of Arbroath the privilege of wearing the mitre, ring and other insignia of a bishop.

1233

UP AND RUNNING
Arbroath's abbey church is dedicated for worship on 8 May 1233, in the 20th year of the reign of Alexander II (right).

1272

STORM DAMAGE
The *Scotichronicon* records a storm that damages Arbroath Abbey's towers, as well as St Andrews Cathedral.

TROUBLESOME ABBOTS

Few particulars are known about the earliest abbots of Arbroath, other than the less-than-happy abbacies of Robert, the eighth abbot, and Henry, the thirteenth. According to the historian Fordun, Robert was expelled by his monks in 1267. He appealed to the pope, but without any success. Henry appears to have been even less popular: in the early 1290s his monks complained to Pope Nicholas IV that Henry harried them 'with the stings of affliction and the bites of persecution'. Henry's position remained secure, however, since he enjoyed the support of King John Balliol.

Above: The Dominican friar St Vincent, shown working in his study. The Tironensian monks placed emphasis on scholastic studies.

THE DECLARATION OF ARBROATH

The single event for which Arbroath is best known is the issuing of the letter known as the Declaration of Arbroath from the abbey on 6 April 1320. Sent on behalf of the nobles of Scotland to Pope John XXII, its extraordinarily eloquent plea for the recognition of Scotland's autonomy continues to resonate today.

One reason for the Declaration was to persuade the pope to lift the sentence of excommunication on Robert I, imposed after Robert's murder of his rival, John Comyn, in a church in Dumfries in 1306. This aim foundered, but another one, that of making the papacy recognise Robert as king of a Scottish nation independent from England, was finally achieved in 1329.

The content of the Declaration was probably agreed at a council held at Newbattle Abbey, Midlothian, in March. The reason it took its final form at Arbroath is quite simply that Abbot Bernard was Robert I's chancellor. From the form of the script, it was clearly written by one of the royal chancery clerks, who was presumably based at Arbroath. Abbot Bernard himself was probably not the author, being neither a graduate nor a diplomat. Possible candidates include Alexander Kinninmund, a future bishop of Aberdeen who was a member of the embassy to the pope, and Walter Twynholm, Bernard's successor as chancellor.

Right: Forty nobles, barons and freemen affixed their seals to the Declaration, urging the pope to recognise Scotland's independence.

1320

THE DECLARATION OF ARBROATH
Abbot Bernard despatches the letter from the abbey to Pope John XXII.

1329

CRY FREEDOM!
King Robert I, on his deathbed, at last receives papal recognition of Scotland's right to independence.

'For as long as but a hundred of us remain alive,
never will we on any condition be brought under English rule.

It is in truth not for glory, nor riches,
nor honours that we are fighting, but for freedom.'

From the Declaration of Arbroath, 1320

DECLINE AND FALL

Few religious communities were able to maintain the highest standards that had been expected of them by their founders. It was the chief irony of monastic life that, while it had been the holiness of the monks' lives that attracted lavish benefactions from those wishing to share in the spiritual benefits of their prayers, those same benefactions made it increasingly difficult for the monks to live up to the original aspirations. Arbroath was no exception.

The need for a general improvement in standards was recognised in 1415 when Pope Benedict XIII ordered Abbot Walter of Arbroath to summon a chapter of Scotland's Benedictine abbots to consider how things might be improved. One problem was the extent of involvement by laypeople in the life of the abbey. In 1425, Abbot Walter himself was employing six secular notaries (legal officers) to help him administer the abbey estates. In addition, the bailie, the official in overall charge of the abbey's regality, was by now usually a leading local layman. By the 15th century, the Ogilvies of Inverquharity saw this lucrative office as their hereditary right.

Above: An early 16th-century carved oak statue of St Mary Magdalene (origin unknown), on display in the abbot's house. The abbey's own religious statues did not survive the Reformation.

1446

A FAMILY QUARREL
The Ogilvies and the Lindsays (whose arms are shown here) argue over which of them should be bailie of Arbroath Abbey.

1560

REFORMATION
The Reformation ends Scotland's ties with Rome and brings monastic life at Arbroath to a close.

Unfortunately another local family, the Lindsays, disagreed, and quarrels ensued. In 1446, a bloody affray was fought out by the two sides. The abbey's great wealth also attracted the attention of other churchmen. In 1470, Patrick Graham, the worldly bishop of St Andrews, imprisoned Abbot Malcolm Brydy for daring to oppose his attempts to extract funds from the abbey.

Above: A decorative timber fitting from the abbot's house.

CROWN APPOINTMENTS

The situation worsened after 1500 when commendators (royal appointees) rather than abbots began to be appointed as heads of the abbey. Whilst some took an interest in the monasteries placed under their care, most simply saw them as a source of income in reward for their services to the crown.

The first commendator of Arbroath was a son of King James III, James duke of Ross, who was appointed in 1503. Following the death of his successor, George Hepburn, at the battle of Flodden in 1513, an unseemly struggle developed, ending in the appointment of an illegitimate son of King James IV, James Stewart, earl of Moray. Various members of the highly acquisitive Beaton family followed. The first, James, archbishop of Glasgow, was eventually succeeded, after another unedifying disagreement, by his nephew David, who became archbishop of St Andrews in 1539. The third Beaton, another James, resigned in 1551 when he became archbishop of Glasgow. The last commendator before the Reformation was John, Lord Hamilton, a son of Regent Arran, who later became first marquis of Hamilton. His descendants would eventually own the estate of the abbey outright.

Above: Cardinal David Beaton, the second of three Beaton family members to hold the office of abbot of Arbroath. Beaton was a hugely important figure in the run-up to the Reformation of 1560, and was murdered at St Andrews Castle in 1546 following his burning of the Protestant preacher, George Wishart.

AFTER THE REFORMATION

The Scottish Reformation of 1560 effectively brought monastic life at Arbroath, as elsewhere, to an end, although the abbey continued to exist as a land–holding corporation under the leadership of its commendator. At least three of the 22 monks then at Arbroath opted to join the reformed Church as ministers. Those who refused were allowed to continue living at the abbey until their death.

Apart from the abbot's house, which probably continued to serve as the commendators' residence, little attempt was made to preserve the rest of the complex. It was not long before the buildings came to be regarded as no more than a useful source of masonry material, and in 1580 stone and timber was taken to build a new church in the burgh, to replace the old parish church at St Vigeans.

Above: The abbey church went rapidly from splendour to ruin, as this 18th-century version of a 1693 engraving graphically shows. The open area in the foreground, to the north and east of the abbey church, was formerly the burial ground of the monks, but by this date was becoming a graveyard for the townspeople.

Early in the 17th century, one visitor to the abbey bemoaned '…the deplorable state of the defaced and staggering steeples, the battered wals, broken doune pillars and the flore al overgrowne with grass and defiled with filth and excrements of unreasonable beasts…' By the time John Slezer published his views of the abbey in 1693, it was already almost as extensively ruined as it is now.

CONSERVING THE PAST

It was not until the early 19th century, however, that the importance of the abbey's remains – both as a noble piece of medieval architecture and for the light they cast upon Scotland's past – came to be appreciated. In 1815 the Barons of the Exchequer, who dealt with crown finances in Scotland, provided funds for conservation works to be carried out. Floor levels inside the church were lowered, leading to the discovery of a fine early 14th-century effigy, believed to be a posthumous commemoration of William I.

Later in the 1800s the process began of removing buildings that had encroached on the monastic precinct, to improve the amenity of the ancient abbey. Today, visitors can learn all about the story of the abbey, its monks and its role in Scotland's past in a splendid exhibition centre adjoining the west front, which opened in 2003.

Below: A detail from one of the post-Reformation tombstones in the graveyard showing Death and an old woman. Death is holding an arrow or 'sting' ('Death, where is thy sting?').

1816	1951

A ROYAL DISCOVERY
A marble effigy thought to represent William the Lion is found during clearance work.

ACT OF PROTEST
Scottish students remove the Stone of Destiny from Westminster Abbey to Arbroath, where they deposit it beside the high altar.

Arbroath Abbey is one of over 20 Historic Scotland sites in Angus, Tayside and North Fife, a selection of which is shown below.

Edzell Castle and Garden

↗ At Edzell, 6m N of Brechin, on the B966

🕐 Open all year **Winter:** closed Thu/Fri

📞 01356 648631

🚗 Approx. 30 miles from Arbroath Abbey

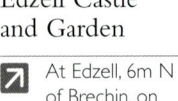

Meigle Sculptured Stone Museum

↗ In Meigle, 6m SE of Glamis, off the A94

🕐 Open summer only. Other times by prior arrangement.

📞 01828 640612

🚗 Approx. 33 miles from Arbroath Abbey

St Andrews Castle

↗ In St Andrews on the A91

🕐 Open all year

📞 01334 477196

🚗 Approx. 30 miles from Arbroath Abbey

St Andrews Cathedral

↗ In St Andrews on the A91

🕐 Open all year

📞 01334 472563

🚗 Approx. 30 miles from Arbroath Abbey

For more information on all Historic Scotland sites, visit **www.historic-scotland.gov.uk**
To order tickets and a wide range of products, visit **www.historic-scotland.gov.uk/shop**

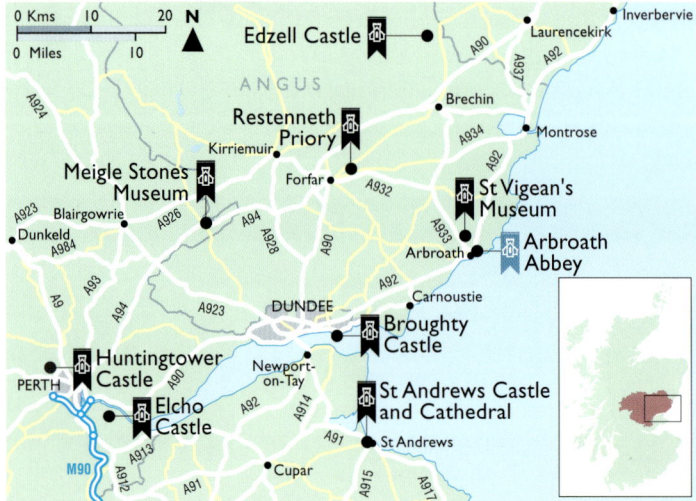

Key to facilities

Visitor centre	𝒊
Admission charge	💷
Bus/coach parking	🚌
Car parking	P
Interpretive display	🎯
Picnic area	🪑
Reasonable wheelchair access	♿
Shop	🛍
Toilets	🚻